SHE'S GOT GAME
THE PLAYBOOK

By
KAYCEE SHERRELLE

SHE'S GOT GAME, THE PLAYBOOK

SHE'S GOT GAME, THE PLAYBOOK

Cover design by Shantrice Looney / Debonair Design
Graphics LLC

Book design by KayCee Sherrelle

First Edition: April 2013
Printed in the United States of America

First Printing: April 2013
Print Tekk Printing and Mailing

ISBN-978-0-9890710-0-0

SHE'S GOT GAME, THE PLAYBOOK

ACKNOWLEDGMENTS

This book would not have been possible without the support, advice and encouragement from Pastor Gary Cornelius Jones. Pastor Jones gave me an initial writing assignment that ignited the spark for this book. Words cannot express my gratitude to Shantrice Looney for her professional advice and assistance in designing the book cover. I would like to thank my children, Jazzalyn, Andrea and Kiona for understanding my long nights at the computer. Lastly, I have to thank all of my friends and colleagues who participated in all of my interviews and surveys.

SHE'S GOT GAME, THE PLAYBOOK

SHE'S GOT GAME, THE PLAYBOOK

Dedicated to my three greatest accomplishments:
Jazzalyn, Andrea and Kiona

SHE'S GOT GAME, THE PLAYBOOK

THE PLAYBOOK

"If the relationship can't survive the long term, why on earth would it be worth my time and energy for the short term?" Nicholas Sparks, The Last Song

INTRODUCTION

"A woman's heart should be so hidden in God that a man has to seek Him just to find her."
Maya Angelou

I have spent the past five years, since my divorce, trying to understand this intricate game that we call dating, and dating encounters with undeserving men who seemed to suck all the energy out of me. This book is a collective sum total of interviews and discussions that I have had with many different women from various social, ethnic and financial backgrounds as well as my own experiences. This is not a book that promotes dishonesty or games; rather, it's a playbook for women to make reference to when needed.

I decided to write this book as an instructional guide to inform and encourage women on how to minimize heartache. This wisdom was not something that I learned out of a textbook or that someone told to me. I learned the playbook of the game from living life each day. Each experience, good or bad, taught me a lifelong lesson that I have to share.

During my journey, I would find myself saying the serenity prayer often. This prayer was written by Reinhold Niebuhr in 1943. Almost seventy years ago! To this day it is still applicable, especially with matters of the heart and the dating game, and it will serve as the fundament basis to all the lessons in your journey. Believe me when I tell you that these following words should be recited to yourself as a daily mantra.

"God grant me the serenity to accept the things I cannot change; courage to change the things I can; and wisdom to

know the difference."

Before we get into the "meat and potatoes" of the schematics of playing the dating game, we as women have to know exactly what we want and be able to identify what love is, and how to nurture the love when we get it. Even though there are no set rules on how to play the dating game, there are guidelines, and I pray that as you read this book, you are entertained and that it will serve as a unique learning tool. Enjoy!

CHAPTER 1

WHAT ARE YOU LOOKING FOR?

What Are You Looking For?

"Do not give dogs what is sacred; do not throw your pearls to pigs. If you do, they may trample them under their feet, and then turn and tear you to pieces." Matthew 7:6

Before you can learn and play the Dating Game effectively, you have to understand and know who you are as a woman. Take some time to do a self evaluation and ask yourself some probing questions. What do you want? What don't you want? What you like about yourself? Where do you have room to improve? We, as women, have to learn how to live alone and get to know ourselves before committing to a relationship. Recognize your worth and don't let any man tell you otherwise.

Have you heard the story from the Bible that talks about "not throwing your pearls before swine?" It is part of a sermon that Jesus told and can be found in the New Testament. To paraphrase: We should not be giving our goods (time, energy, money, love, etc.) to anybody or any situation that does not appreciate or acknowledge them. Recognize your worth and make him EARN the right to be with you. Real talk ladies, men will say anything to get into your panties. Instead of believing everything that a man is telling you, look at what they do. Do their actions match their words? Don't play yourself, the more confident and independent you are, the more they will chase you. You don't have to be cold- hearted or callous and treat men negatively, just take the necessary steps to protect your heart.

Sometimes in order to discover what you want, you have to discover what you don't want and unfortunately for

15

some women that takes real life experience. I know because I lived it. Every story or example in this book is something that I lived and had to learn the hard way. I don't want my daughters or anybody else's daughters to have to go through any unnecessary heartache pain. I did not have anybody to teach me the Dating Game, and what to look out for, and what to stay away from. I had no idea what red flags were until after I had been through a few traumatic situations. It's my prayer that the readers come out a lot wiser at the end of the book, than they did at the first page.

Every woman that I know, with myself included, has a list of qualities that we desire in a mate. Try this exercise out. Make a list of qualities that you want in a mate, then make a list of some qualities that you don't really like, but are willing to live with. Remember, no man is going to be perfect. Every woman is different with different desires, so your list may not match up completely with mine or with any other woman that you know. Based on conversations that I have had with women over the years and my own wants, I compiled a list of the top qualities that most women want in a man:

> Number One: **Be Available**.   You have to be SINGLE. By single I mean, not MARRIED. If I ask you if you are married and your answer is "No" and then I find out later that you lied, that is an automatic vote off of the island. Single means: being completely available to date and be seen out in public with a woman with no restrictions.

> Number Two: **A relationship with God**. The man has to have his own personal relationship with God. How can you have a relationship with another human, if you don't have a personal relationship

16

with God? If a man has a close relationship with God, then most of the qualities on this list are going to automatically be included in his personality make-up.

Number Three: **Honesty.** Being up front and honest is so vital. This is pretty high up on the list too. No one wants to be lied to and if you start a relationship off by lying, then the foundation is going to be weak, and whatever relationship or "structure" that you build on top of lies will surely not last. Respect and trust is gained a lot quicker in the relationship with honesty. When lies are exposed (and they usually are) there will always be this doubt. You will always think in the back of your mind whether that man is telling the truth. Once you are busted in a lie, every word out of your mouth is questionable. It simply is not worth it. Relationships should have a strong foundation that is built on trust.

Number Four: **Faithfulness.** For some reason, some men think that they can get away with cheating and it does not affect them. There is no excuse for being unfaithful. Once that line is crossed, there is no turning back and your relationship will never be the same again.

Number Five: **Sense of Humor**. I am not saying that a man has to be Chris Rock, just someone who has a sense of humor to make you laugh on a regular basis. Laughter can be the best medicine for you when you are having a bad day and it can diffuse a negative situation.

Number Six: **Commitment**. This is a key

component for a long term relationship. Without commitment, there is always going to be doubt in the back of a woman's mind about the seriousness of the relationship. Ask yourself questions like: Do his actions show me that he loves me like he says that he does? Is he going to be around in six months? How long is he going to be around? Do I even want him around in the long term?

Number Seven: **The ability to protect.** Women want a man who can protect her if needed, including physically in dangerous situations. That does not mean that the man is walking around town beating his chest with his fist. Or picking fights to prove how tough he is. He just must be able to handle a physical altercation if needed.

Number Eight: **Reliability.** Do what you say that you are going to do. Women love men who keep their word, who let women know that they can count on a man. This helps to build trust.

Number Nine: **Respect.** Without respect, there is no relationship. Not only do men have to respect women, men have to respect themselves. Respecting the level of commitment in the relationship is also very important. Knowing and respecting the level of commitment is of the utmost importance because it sets boundaries and guidelines for the Rules of Engagement. Now, you may be asking yourself, what exactly are the rules of engagement? We will discuss that topic later in section five.

Number Ten: **Attractiveness.** This is an inner

quality that a person is born with and is something that is based on one's personal tastes. Every woman has a certain attractive feature that they like. Personally, for me, I like the type of man that can groom himself well and be confident in who he is as a man.

Number Eleven: **In tune with feelings**. Women need men to be in tune with their feelings. Men need to be in tune with their own feelings as well. Women are emotional creatures and they have to have their feelings validated. Validating a woman's feelings does not mean that a man must agree with what a woman is feeling. It simply means that he understands what she is feeling and why she may feel that way.

Number Twelve: **Belief in her**. A man who is going to support a woman's dreams and give her encouragement is very important.

Number Thirteen: **Motivation**. Women don't like men who have no "get up and go." Women want men that have passion and goals. A plan of action on how to achieve them is a definite plus.

Number Fourteen: **Social Etiquette**. You have to have social etiquette. Any man that a woman is seen out in public with, or that she takes around her family, must know how to behave in public. There is no way that she is going to be publicly embarrassed by someone with uncouth behavior. When she is on a date eating dinner; the bill may come and a man may look at her like, "Do you want me to pay for your meal too?" Which, in turn, makes her eyes say to him: "I wish I could. Please, you invited me out." Also, no tipping at the end of a meal is a major turn off. If a man does not know how to tip, then that's really sad. If he doesn't have enough money to tip, then a woman should question his ability to manage his finances.

Number Fifteen: **Fiscal Maturity**. The man has to have the ability to manage his finances and adhere to a budget. Not having fiscal maturity is a turn off.

Number Sixteen: **Leadership and Management**. This goes back to the first quality on the list. Think about it. The man in the relationship is supposed to be the leader. Now that does not mean that he has the right to degrade or belittle his woman. It just means that he is in a leadership role that is right under God. If a man has a personal relationship with God, then he is going to turn to God to guide his path, which, in turn, is going to lead you and his family down the right road in life. Women need a man with both leadership and management skills. Some men can lead and some can just manage. Some can do both. It takes a special man to be able to do both.

Ladies, please stop thinking that every man that you meet is your King. You may meet a man that has most of the characteristics on your list, and he still may not be the one. Take your time and really get to know these men before you give your love, time, emotions, and body (your goods) to them. Be particularly careful with your body. A lot of times we as women get caught up with the idea of being in love with a man just from having sex with him, because it feels good and we have not been caressed or touched like that in a while. Then, when it happens, we tend to get caught up in the emotion of it all and equate sex with love.

The need for the human touch can be a powerful thing. During sex the human body releases a hormone that tells our brains that "This makes me feels good" and "I like it." Most women are unaware of Oxytocin. Oxytocin is the hormone that stimulates pleasure in the brain and is often call the "love hormone" and is associated with lust. This love hormone unfortunately can sometimes cause a woman to stay in a dysfunctional relationship, even when she knows that it's wrong. Ignoring those pangs of conscience in the pit or her stomach tends to put a woman in potentially dangerous situations. When your brain is clouded by lust, it can be extremely difficult to make rational decisions. Too much pure emotion without a balance of logic is definitely a recipe for disaster.

Learn how to love with your eyes wide open, and be aware of exactly who you are dealing with. Sit down and make a list of pros and cons. Sometimes, there can be ten good things about a man and only two bad things, but those two bad things can outweigh the good things. Learn how to love cautiously. Learn to use both your heart and mind to judge if something is real. Learning to love logically is not easy for some women to do. Basically guard your heart. Your heart is the source from where your life flows. Everybody at some point in life is going to get his or her heart broken. It's a part of life. I learned how to guard by getting it broken a few times and giving my heart to God to protect.

Whenever you sincerely pray to God for the protection of your heart, he does just that. God's protection is like a force field and no harm can come your way.

Whatever negative or painful intentions that a man or anybody else tries to inflict on you will bounce right off. My heart does not have to feel the heartache pain anymore because Jesus died on the cross and endured every pain and sickness known and unknown to man. I still feel the protection from God around my heart, and I know that no man is ever going to hurt me again, because he is going to have to go through God just to get to me. Loving with your eyes wide open and continually praying to God to protects your heart and helps to minimize baggage. Baggage will only drag you down and cause you think that every man is going to treat you the same. That is not true. Men, like women, are different. All men do not act or think the same. I start every man that I consider dating with an automatic "A" and it is up to him to maintain it. This can help to prevent bringing excess baggage from past relationships into a new one.

Every man that you meet is not going to abuse and mistreat you. If you find yourself attracting the same type of men, do an examination of your inner-self, asking yourself what is the most common dominator in your past relationships? The answer is you! You have to change things within yourself to attract a different type of man and, if who you are does not fit with who he is don't force it. Just move on, because you could miss out on a special relationship wasting time with the wrong person. In short, learn how to love yourself most of all, because you cannot love anybody else unless you love yourself first.

CHAPTER 2

DEFINING YOUR LOVE

Defining Your Love

"So it's not gonna be easy. It's going to be really hard; we're gonna have to work at this every day, but I want to do that because I want you. I want all of you, forever, every day. You and me... every day."
Nicholas Sparks, The Notebook

Do you really know what love is? Love is a growth process, and it takes time. You plant the initial seed the first time that you meet a man and realize that there is some chemistry there. You find yourself drawn to that person as if you were magnets. Before you go on your quest for love, take some time to do an internal evaluation. In order to love someone else, you have to do two fundamental things:

1) **Love yourself**. Know who you are as a person. What you like; what you don't like. What are you limits in a relationship? What are your deal-breakers and non-issues? What are you going to put up with, and what would make you leave a man?

2) **Discover what kind of lover that you are**. The look of love can be different between two people. Recognizing what kind of lover that you are is essential. You have to know what kind of lover you are, so that you can match yourself up with someone with a similar definition. You may see yourself in one of the definitions below or a combination.

Are you the Romantic lover? In love with romanticism and the idea of being in love? You often find yourself getting swept off your feet by your lover's appearance. When they no longer have the same outward appeal, you lose interest. Perhaps you are the lover that has very high standards. The List-Maker has a list a mile long full of standards that are almost too high. That super long list of "must-do's" may lead you to a lifetime of loneliness. After all, no man is going to be perfect.

The Independent Lover is the type of lover that often finds herself in relationships where her needs do not get met. Not because her man is not trying, but because she won't give him a chance. Give a man an opportunity to help you out if he can. She cannot get upset with him for not helping her out in a crisis, if he has no idea of what is going on. Or you are the obsessive type. You are so obsessed with what your lover is doing or not doing that you want to know what he is doing all time. This insecurity can drive you to want to consume all your lover's time so that you can keep an eye on him. It doesn't matter if you have been together for a few months or a few years. Watch out! That is suffocating, and is a recipe that can drive your lover away. Remember, you are his mate not his mother.

You might be so giving of yourself and love your partner so much that you neglect your own needs. The Giver type of lover's whole life revolves around her lover's needs and wants. Don't get so caught up in your lover's life that you stop taking care of yours. Maybe you are at a time in your life where you just want to play the field. The Player type of lover does not want to settle down. She is perfectly content with dating numerous men with no commitment. There is nothing wrong with that. We as women go through different phases in our lives and sometimes settling down is not what we want to do. Back in my player days, I was dating (not having sex with) five to six men at any given time. I would go to breakfast, lunch, and dinner with a different man. Just be honest with every man that you are involved with. When you first meet a man, there is nothing wrong with letting a man know that he has competition.

Knowing who you are and what kind of lover that you are is essential in the dating process. When I love someone, I tend to love hard and give a hundred and ten percent. The old me used to fall in love too fast. I was so fixated with being in love and not being alone that I would just settle down with any man. The new me is confident in who I am and not afraid of not being in a relationship. My life experiences have taught me to slow down and take my time to really get to know a man before I just react on pure emotion alone.

CHAPTER 3

THE THREE TYPES OF LOVE

The Three Types of Love

"Love is patient, love is kind. It does not envy, it does not boast, it is not proud. It does not dishonor others, it is not self-seeking, it is not easily angered. It keeps no record of wrongs. Love does not delight in evil but rejoices with the truth. It always protects, always trusts always hopes, always preserves." 1 Corinthians 13:4-7 NIV

There are three types of love or levels in the love process. Understanding the three types of love is fundamental in establishing a long-lasting relationship. The three types of love are:

Eros love. Otherwise known, as the "erotic love." It is a love based on strong physical feelings toward another. It's the chemistry factor and it usually occurs in the first stages of a man and woman "romantic" relationship. It is what attracts men and women to each other. Very few people fall "in love at first sight." When two people feel this type of strong emotional attraction towards one another too soon, they will usually put their best feet forward and only show their good sides as representatives of who they are. How can two people feel this strength of emotions when they barely know each other? For true love to exist, the man and the woman have to know and accept each other for both their good and bad qualities.

This type of love is weak, because it is a "self-fulfilling" kind of love. The focus is more on what makes you feel good. Often times you will hear people say "Loving you feels good and makes me happy." The keyword is "ME." When a person doesn't have that happy feeling anymore in loving someone, he or she can be led to

31

believe that they have "fallen out of love." Realistically, they never were truly "in love" in the first place. You and your potential mate have to spend a lot of time together. Sharing memories together of both pains and pleasures and still staying together is a mark of genuine love. If a love is not tested by hardships it usually does not last long term. A relationship has a better chance of lasting and developing into the next stage of philos love with ups and downs. Eros love has to progress gradually over time into the next step of love in order to last, otherwise it will fizzle out. Eros love is a natural and important part of any romantic relationship. Eros love is romantic and part of God's plan. It plays a vital role in the strengthening the bonds, especially at the beginning of a relationship.

Philos love. A love based on deep rooted friendship between two people. It is often said that lovers that start out as being friends first before committing to a relationship are the ones that usually last the longest. Friendship is the fundamental foundation of a long lasting and successful relationship. This can be applied to any relationship; Marriage, boyfriend/girlfriend, relationship between co-workers, family, etc.

In dealing with a man-woman romantic relationship, it would be advantageous to get to know each other first before you progress to a more serious type of relationship. You have to start out as friends first; highly recommended without sex. Spending time together; admiring each other and then the stronger emotions can appear over time. Eventually, you will both realize that you start to miss each other more and more. It is going to take time and patience. Philos love is totally different from Eros love because it is based on a mutual "give and "take attitude which can allow two people to benefit from each other in a mutual way, creating a "win-win" relationship.

Both partners are concerned with what they can get out of the relationship, and yet at the same time deeply concerned with his or her partner's benefit. This is strikingly different from Eros love. With Eros love you can only see the other persons' good side (their strengths). Everything is perfect, and you get a feeling of happiness. You are more attracted to a person's physical or mental traits alone. You don't really know them enough to form real love emotions. You are blinded by lust. You cannot judge real love based on lust and strong emotions alone. Philos love is higher than Eros love. Philos is a love based on "give and take" and Eros is a love based on self benefit. Just like Eros love, philos love has to develop into the highest stage of love. Agape, or unconditional love.

Agape. The highest form of love and is above both Eros and philos love. It is the type of love that is completely selfless. This type of love is what urges some people to go out of their way to do an act of love for another person with absolutely no benefit for themselves in any way. It does not matter if the love that is given is returned or not, they will continue to love, even without any benefits to themselves. Examples can be: helping someone out, even when that person does not like you and is always mean to you; it's the kind of unconditional love that a mother has for her children. A man could be on trial for murder. His mother is going to come to court every day showing her love and support to her child, even when she knows that he is guilty; the kind of love that we show our parents when they get older; taking care of them when they are ill, without expecting any benefit in return, the same way that they took care of us when we were growing up.

What is unique about agape love is that it is not a human love at all. It's God's love for us. God's love for us is unconditional because we are his children. God showed us how much he loved us when he sent his only son, Jesus Christ, to die on the cross for our sins. There is no greater love than this, because Jesus did not have to die for our salvation. He chose to do so. He gave his life so that we could have an everlasting life. Jesus gave us his ultimate gift, his life.

Ever since the first sin in the Garden of Eden by Adam and Eve, mankind has become riddled with so much sin that no one could redeem himself on his own. Even if every person suffered and died on the cross, like Jesus did, it would still not be enough to repay all the debts of sins to God. Jesus loved us so much that even when he was on the cross, he prayed to God to forgive us. That is real unconditional love. In the Bible, First Corinthians 13:4-8 tells us exactly what agape love is. Love never fails.

To sum everything up: Eros love is a physical type of love that is based on physical attraction. Philos love is a mental type of love that is based on the mind. Agape love is a spiritual type of love that is based on God. This makes up the three basic elements of mankind: physical, mental, and spiritual. Now that you know what you want and can identify the three types of love, it is time to use your "tools" (knowledge) to effectively play the dating game.

The goal is not to play the game for you to be the only winner. The goal is to play the game to create a "win-win" situation for you and your potential mate. It's a trust in believing the other person when they tell you "I love you." Loving someone and being in love with someone are two different things. You can have love in your heart for a man and not be in love with him. Love, is a growth process that takes time to flourish into something genuine. So take your time and be patient.

CHAPTER 4

THE GAME

WHAT IS GAME?

What is Game?

"Don't hate the player, hate the game"
Ice-T

We have all heard the above mentioned quote by Ice-T on several occasions. I am going to teach you the Rules of Engagement (explained later) and how to play the dating game with minimal heartache. Every woman that I know has a list in her head about what characteristics that they want in a man. Well, men are the same way. They have a list of character traits that they want in a woman.

Women who know the game and who have their lives in order are a rare breed. Men know that they don't run into a diva on a daily basis. So when they find one, they do whatever they can to make her happy and keep her happy, so that she won't leave and take her "Nectar" with her and give it to another man. Smile. The secret to your happiness is you. The power is yours. All you need is the mental tools to get it done. The power that you need is inside you. It's a gift that God gave you. Time to roll up your sleeves, take notes and get to work!

This section will serve as a foundation for the lessons in remaining topics of this playbook. We will focus on developing the necessary skills to keep your heart safe. When it comes to dating, every woman should never expect, demand, or assume anything. A woman should always know her limits, that is, here she stands, and what her role is in the relationship.

Don't get affected, jealous or paranoid about anything. More importantly go with the flow and choose to be happy. Remember, happiness is a choice that we make every day. This section will encompass the following in detail: How to be a Furniture Mover, The Mental Blueprint, Red Flags, Bottom Feeders and Deal Breakers. You will also learn about male dating behaviors, the basic thought processes of a men and why they lie so much! Hopefully, with your new found knowledge you will be better equipped to know exactly how to play the dating game to create a win-win situation.

First off, men are hunters. They thrive on the chase. The faster you run, the faster they will chase you. Trust me. Billy Crystal said it best, "Women need a reason to have sex; men just need a place." So use it and not abuse it to your advantage. Even after reading this book and learning the game, you still need to live your life with integrity and class. Remember to always carry yourself like a Lady and not a Hoe. No woman should want to leave a bad taste in any man's mouth.

The unknown secret to understanding a man in the dating realm is that most men are afraid of rejection. Because men are afraid of rejection, they will usually only approach a woman if she has given him noticeable signal. For example: you are sitting down at a restaurant or nightclub and you notice a nice looking man across the room. He may have seen you when you walked into the room, however, he is usually not going to make a move until you give him a green light. Well, if he's a Bottom Feeder he might, and you don't want one of those on your team anyway.

The best green light to give is eye contact. Look around the room and assess they layout. Find the bathrooms and nonchalantly walk past him heading that way. Make sure and pause slightly in front of him, smile, look him in the eye and say, "Excuse me." This will give the man the subtle hint that you might be interested in getting to know him. The key word is might. You don't want to come off too strong too early in the game. Let him question and wonder whether you were being flirtatious or merely being polite. Even though you noticed him first, you have to let him think that he noticed you first. Otherwise, everything will be off-balance and he will think that you are chasing him.

When you meet a man, the first thought in his mind is not how smart you are. Nor is it the brand of clothes that you have on. Hell, he doesn't care if you have on any clothes at all. You could be wearing a potato sack and a man's x-ray vision eyes will penetrate right through the material in about 30 seconds. He wants a taste of your Nectar. Men want what you walk around with everyday. Yes Ladies, men are simple Creatures. It's we women that are the complicated ones. If you give him a taste too soon, he is not going to respect you. The thrill of the chase will be gone, and so will the man. You should value yourself and your nectar to a high regard. Not every man deserves a taste. It takes a unique skill to use this information to your advantage. It's more mental than anything else. With guidance and practice, you too will learn exactly what to do. You will be a professional "Furniture Mover."

Before I explain exactly what a Furniture Mover is, let me give you the background of where the phrase originated. Long before I had learned the game, on one sunny afternoon, my cousin Binks and I were out at a local bar enjoying a few cocktails. As we were sipping our drinks, one of the older gentlemen named Ray, who was sitting at the bar, got up from his seat and came over to where we were and said, "We got two professional furniture movers in here today." Binks and I looked at each other with confusion and laughed at each other. Smiling, we, turned our heads and looked at Ray for clarification. So I asked "Ray, what are you talking about?" Ray's reply was, "Well, you are two beautiful young ladies who have their heads on straight. So I know that you are moving all kinds of furniture around in men's heads. I bet that you can get any man to do anything that you want him to do, by just asking. Ya'll don't even know the power that you have. One day you're are going figure it out, and when you do, they better watch out!"

We walked out of the bar and laughed Ray's words off as if he was joking, or the Crown Royal that he was drinking was influencing his words. At that particular time I had no idea what he was referring to. Me? A furniture mover? What was he alking about? Little did I know that those words that Ray told me that day were going to plant a seed and provide a path to my learning and implementing the Game.

Furniture moving is an art. It requires the practice of the Jedi Mind Trick; and knowing the mental blueprint of the man's mind is also essential. The purpose is to make the man think the idea in his head is one that he came up with, when actually, you are the one who put the idea there in the first place. When carefully chosen words are implanted into the male mind, all you have to do is provide verbal water (words) and watch them grow.

An example would be: You don't like the company that he keeps. One of his male friends is a notorious whore. You know it, and his friend knows that you know. Ya'll do not get along for three simple reasons: You don't like him, he don't like you, and ya'll don't like each other. Since his friend is a whore and always trying to encourage your man to engage in whore-like behavior, his interaction has to be cut down significantly.

Now you know that you can't come right out and tell your man not to talk to his friend anymore. Instead, casually mention that his "Boy" was looking at you, and it made you feel uncomfortable. Say something like: "Wow, your friend has really unique eyes. The last time I saw him, he was staring right at me with a strange smile on his face. It kind of made me feel weird." Then change the subject quickly, and walk out of the room, or hang the phone up.

Those simply chosen words will seep deep into his membrane and start to manifest. Long after the conversation he will still be thinking about what you said, and the next time that he sees his friend, your words will replay in his head. Your man will come up with the only logical solution that he can think of for why his friend is looking at his woman like that. Your man is going to say to himself, "My Boy wants my woman!" With that new found revelation, his friend's presence will diminish dramatically.

Learning the Mental Blueprints of men takes time and patience. It involves asking pertinent questions and being observant. Pay close attention to what they like and don't like. Learning what their habits and routines are is necessary. Most importantly, you have to do less talking. Keep your mouth closed so that you can hear what is being said, and more importantly, what's not being said. Often times it's the missing words that will provide you with the most information. There is no set time frame of how long it is going to take to learn the Blueprint. Take your time and really get to know him. The Blueprint is an intangible and valuable tool to have in any relationship.

Knowing the Mental Blueprint early in the game will help you to identify what a Red Flag is. Being able to spot Red Flags is necessary to keep you from wasting your precious time on a Bottom Feeder. Red Flags are negative character traits that some men have. Also keep in mind that every woman's tolerance level is different. Like most things, it's subjective. To be subjective to all the demographics of everyone reading this book, I have compiled a list in no particular order, of the top ten things that I would consider to be Red Flags:

Number One: **He has ill regard for his own family**. Let's use his mother as an example. Any man that is mean to his mother, and has nothing nice to say about her is not the man for you. Regardless of his childhood, or what she did to him; the fact that he is standing alive in front of you is something that he should at least be grateful for. Giving him life was a gift that she did not have to do. He could at least be grateful for that.

Number Two: **You have not been invited into his personal world.** You've dated for several months and haven't met any of his friends, family or co-workers. This usually indicates that he has a wife or a girlfriend somewhere, and it's not you. Or he has numerous women.

Number Three: **He ignores you.** He sometimes won't answer your phone calls or return your texts. Which is a major pet peeve of mine.

Number Four: **His ex is still in the picture.** Especially annoying; when they do not have any children together, thus having no real reason to talk all the time.

Number Five: **Little or no involvement with his children**. He has a child(ren) that he "doesn't see that much." He rarely talks about them, and they live in the same city.

Number Six: **He is inept**. He doesn't know how to do laundry, mop a floor, clean a tub, or cook a simple dinner. A major indication that he is extremely lazy or a Momma's boy, and you will have to take care of him.

Number Seven: **He has multiple children.** By multiple women, and all of his children are young.

Number Eight: **He never invites you to his place.** What's he hiding? He most likely lives with his mother, his woman, or he is married.

Number Nine: **He has no manners.** He doesn't hold the door, help you with your coat, walk you to the car, etc.

Number Ten: **He is not handling his business**. He has no job, no car, no goals, and no money. He is a Bottom Feeder.

A Bottom Feeder is an aquatic animal that lives and feeds off of the scum at the bottom of the ocean. A Bottom Feeder man is the type of man that is at the bottom of the dating pool ocean. They lack morals, values, and integrity. Bottom Feeders can quickly be identified by the way that they talk. If you meet a man and right away he is talking about sex. That's a pretty good indicator that he is a Bottom Feeder. Ask yourself: "Why is he telling me how he can make my body feel good, and we have not even shared a meal together?" Bottom Feeders will suck the energy out of you if you let them. They are not worthy of your time and energy. Bottom Feeder men are notorious for committing horrible Deal Breaker acts.

Deal breakers are things that men do that break the relationship to a point of no repair. An example of a Deal Breaker is when your man impregnates another woman. Or your man decides that he is going to put his hands on you, by punching you in the face. Some things you can forgive and still have to walk away from. Keep in mind that every woman is different, and one woman's red flag is another woman's deal-breaker and a third woman's non-issue.

WHY DO MEN LIE?

Why Do Men Lie?

"Men are liars. We'll lie about lying if we have to. I'm an algebra liar. I figure two good lies make a positive. "
Tim Allen

All Bottom Feeder men are liars. Yet, men that lie are not necessarily Bottom Feeders. I cannot make an absolute statement, or prove that all men tell lies. I can only affirm that all the men that I know, regardless of age, race, or income status have the tendency to tell lies to women that they profess to love and care about.

During my research on this particular topic, I interviewed many men. I went on a quest to find out what was the reasoning behind the lies that they were telling to women. I know that as humans we are all going to tell lies on occasion, so that was nothing new. I wanted to probe deeper so I decided to talk to a variety of different men about this particular subject. Some of the men I knew personally, like my uncle, brother, close friends, and co-workers. Some were random men that I would encounter at various places. I asked all of them the same questions and, amazingly, I got basically the same answers. I have compiled a list of the top common reasons why men lie to women.

Number One: **To make their woman happy**. Yes ladies, it's true. Men honestly think that they are somehow protecting our feelings by lying to us. Honestly, some of the questions that we ask men are setups for them to lie to us. For example: You ask your man, "How do I look in this dress?" You know that the dress is a little too tight for you, yet you squeezed your size twelve body into a size ten dress. You look in the mirror and even you notice the muffin top around your midsection. If you are dealing with a smart man, his answer is going to be, "You look beautiful as always." What he really wanted to say was, "You look okay, even though I prefer a flatter stomach." We women know that his first answer is a small lie, but we like to hear it, and will happily take it as the truth.

Number Two: **To avoid an argument**. Everybody has different opinions and is not always going to agree on the same things. When people insist on their own opinions, arguments are likely to happen. Too many arguments can become exhausting, and be too much for the male mind to handle. So often the best way for a man to avoid conflict in small matters is by pretending that he agrees with you. Basically, to shut you up.

Number Three: **To justify himself**. Just like women, men will make will mistakes, but they often hate to admit it because they do not want to look bad in front of you. Men think that telling little "harmless" lies here and there will get them out of trouble and keep their good image in your eyes.

Number Four: **To make himself seem better**. Men always value their pride. They want to be the heroes, and want their women to be proud of them. With a "little" lie, they think that women will appreciate them more and feel better for having them around.

Number Five: **To get away with something**. At times men may lie to get something out of you, or to get you to do something for them. It may also be a way to get out of doing something they don't want to do. A lie is a lot easier to say, than explaining the real reasons, and it can be a lot more acceptable, too. The belief that "Sometimes it's better to ask for forgiveness, than to ask for permission."

Men and women process emotions differently. Women are able to feel several emotions at the same time. It's a gift from God! Think of it like a bowl of spaghetti. All of the spaghetti noodles are mixed in together. Not only can we feel all these emotions, we can tell exactly how we feel and why we are feeling that way. Men's emotions are like waffle squares. They only process one emotion at a time. If by chance they do feel more than one emotion at the same time, they will shut down and go into their "Man Cave" until they can sort out their feelings. The Man Cave is that mental place that men go to in order to sort out all the thoughts that are going on in their heads. They pull one emotion out and deal with it before moving on to the next one. Once they have all their feelings sorted out, they will emerge feeling somewhat victorious.

If you are a man and reading this, please understand that we women do know about your lies most of the time, but we either find if mildly amusing, or have no time or energy to get you to come clean. Don't lie too much, or you might just get in serious trouble one day. Ladies, men are going to lie to you at some point. It is just a fact of life. I personally think that men are genetically wired to tell lies. Don't stress too much about little lies that he is telling you. Instead, insist on having good communication and honest talk when you are discussing serious matters. Always pick and choose your battles wisely, because you will not win all of them.

One time I was having an argument with my boyfriend about who he picked up from the airport. I was mildly irritated because I was ninety-nine percent sure that he blew me off at the last minute to hang out with one of his friends. Our conversation went like this:

> Me: "When is your friend leaving? Is he going to need a ride back to the airport?"

> Him: "What are you talking about? Why would he need a ride to airport? He lives here."

> Me: "That is strange, because you told me last night on the phone that you had to go to the airport to pick a friend up who was flying into town for a visit; you wanted to spend some time with him and that was the reason why we could not go to dinner."

> Him: "Honey, that's not what I said. You must have misunderstood. I said that I was picking a friend up from the airport and giving him a ride home. I think that sometimes you have trouble hearing what I am saying when we are on the phone because of my accent."

Now I know what I heard, and it was not his version. I could have handled that situation in one of two ways. I could have continued to badger him until we were both angry and he retreated into his Man Cave, or let it go. I had no hard evidence and yes, he created doubt in my mind. He had one valid reason: he does have an accent, and sometimes I do have difficulty understanding all the words that he is saying. I had to let that minor issue go. It was a non-issue that did not need any more of my time or energy, and for some reason I found the whole conversation slightly amusing, so I decided to give him a pass.

Don't stress too much about little lies that he is telling you. Instead, insist on having good communication and honest talk when you are discussing serious matters. Always pick and choose your battles wisely, because you will not win all of them.

CHAPTER 5

THE RULES OF ENGAGEMENT

Rules of Engagement

"You are remembered for the rules that you break."
Douglas MacArthur

The Rules of Engagement, according to *Business Dictionary.com* is defined as: "Practices followed or behavior displayed by the participants (players) in situations of opposing interests (conflicts) such as negotiations. Unwritten rules of engagement determine what information is given, at what time, to whom, and in what manner; and what concession is granted and what is demanded in return." A set of unwritten verbal rules that both parties decide to agree on in order to maintain a harmonious environment for each person involved.

Relationships are going to change over time, and with changes in the relationship the Rules of Engagement will have to adapt also. Keep in mind that when you change the rules of engagement, you cannot get upset when the other person follows suit or makes changes to the rules themselves. There are three core Rules of Engagement which should be followed:

Don't put your hands on me. Keep your negative rough hands to yourself. I like soft touches and kind hands. Ladies, please don't ever allow any man to inflict any type of physical pain on you. Not only are these types of men bottom feeders, they are narcissistic in nature, and you are worth so much more than that.

Don't do anything to me, that you don't want me doing to you. Treat me the way that you want me to treat you. It's the Golden Rule. Do unto me what you want me to do unto you.

Do what you say that you are going to do. You words are so important. That is why you have to make every word count. If you say that you are going to do something, then I am going to hold you to it. Yes men, it is as simple as a phone call. A woman would rather look at her phone and see a missed call than no call at all.

BOUNDARIES
AND
EXPECTATIONS

Boundaries and Expectations

"Boundaries are to protect life, not to limit pleasure."
Edwin Louis Cole

Every relationship that you have, regardless of the nature, has to have boundaries. Boundaries are defined on Wikipedia as: *"Guidelines, rules, or limits that a person creates to identify for themselves what are reasonable, safe, and permissible ways for other people to behave around them, and how they will respond when someone steps outside those limits."* In short, boundaries define the relationship between you and everybody around you. Boundaries are essential because they help us to create a healthy self and aid in creating our personal destinies. They allow us to take responsibility for our actions and knowingly accept the consequences or the benefits of the choices that we make. Boundaries also let us communicate to others to do the same for themselves.

Without any boundaries, people will often feel like they are being taken advantage of, and sometimes will get the message that their needs and feelings have no merit. You should incorporate your own boundaries and expectations from the Rules of Engagement. The following are my personal relationship boundaries:

Number One**: Guard your heart.** This is the number one rule. Even the bible tells us in Proverbs 4:23, "Above all else, guard your heart, for it is the wellspring of life." This verse is telling us to be extremely careful about who we give our "goods" (affection, love, etc.) to. Our heart influences everything else that is going on in our lives. The source of everything that you do in your life flows

63

from your heart. Stay in touch with who you are. Take time to stop, think, and listen to your inner voice to avoid being so wrapped up in the relationship that you cannot see it clearly. Commit with caution learn to love with your eyes wide open. Be aware of the balance of your commitment level, and that the level of commitment is mutual. Don't allow yourself to be in a situation where, in your, mind you are in a relationship, and in his mind you are not.

Number Two: **You are known by the company that you keep.** I am Christian and an upstanding member of the community. Therefore, I cannot be seen around town with a known "street pharmacist" (drug dealer) or any other degenerate man (bottom feeder). "Bad company corrupts good character." 1 Corinthians 15:33. We can sometimes devolve into picking up bad habits by the company that we keep.

Number Three: **Communication.** Talk. Talk. Talk. Communication is so vital in any type of relationship. It is fundamental in the progression of a romantic type of relationship. Without talking to your mate about conflicts, there will be no resolution. Talk about everything. Discuss scars from past relationships and childhoods so that you have a better understanding of whom you are dealing with. This lets you know where the other person is in their healing process. For example: It is not wise to get too romantically involved with someone who is recently divorced, because there is a healing process that a person has to go through in order to properly move on.

Number Four: **The probationary period.** Enforce the probationary period during the first ninety days of getting to know a man before you commit yourself to him emotionally and physically. Take time to really get to know him. Ask pertinent questions so that you can learn his Mental Blue Print. If an employer is going to give you 90 days to prove yourself, don't you think that you are worth the same consideration? Pay attention to signs of sincerity, even the little ones. Does he keep his word? Does he respect you and your values? Don't blame yourself if he proves to you that he is not trustworthy.

During the probationary period ask pertinent questions that are a must-know and don't be ashamed about asking them either. There is nothing wrong with asking a man if he is current on his taxes and child support. Or what the status is on his student loans. If you are a marriage-minded woman, then you better be asking questions early in the probationary period. Trust me, whatever government debt that he has, you will surely take on if you marry him. How will you know if you don't ask?

Number Five: **The background check**. Please do an investigative background check on every man that you consider dating. The world is way too dangerous nowadays to just believe anything that a man tells you. Run the man's name through your local, state and federal fugitive website. Don't forget to check the sexual predator list.

Number Six: **Watch actions for acceptance of**

responsibility. Be observant of the method of conflict resolution. Does he display narcissistic behavior by using unfair tactics to win an argument, and try to belittle you or wear you down? Does he avoid problems? How well does he listen to you? Do your feelings have merit? How does he resolve conflict? During an argument, is your mate going to punch his fist through the wall? Or is he going to sit down like a reasonably thinking adult and talk in a civilized manner?

Number Seven: **No control freaks or "bug-a-boos."** I am grown woman and I do NOT need any man controlling my every move like I am a child. I control what I do with my time, so don't expect a "play-by-play" itinerary of my day as I am doing activities. Give me some room to breathe, and we can touch base with each other sporadically during the day on an "as needed" basis. Please do not call me excessively so soon after we meet. It is annoying and suffocating. That kind of behavior is a sign that the man is excessively needy.

Number Eight: **We must have the same morals and values.** In other words we have to be like-minded and equally-yoked spiritually. If a woman leads a Christian life style then, dating a man that lives an opposite lifestyle is not going to work.

Number Nine: **Honesty and Respect.** Demand to be treated with respect and honesty from the very beginning; pay close attention to his response. Be observant of how a man treats you when you are out in public.

According to the book *Boundaries and Relationships* by Charles Whitfield, M.D., Healthy boundaries are NOT:

- Set for us by others
- Hurtful or harmful
- Controlling or manipulative
- Invasive or dominating
- Rigid and immovable

Healthy boundaries ARE:

- Present
- Appropriate
- Clear
- Firm
- Protective
- Flexible
- Receptive
- Determined by US

Expectations are different than boundaries. Boundaries are rules that can be applicable in every relationship that I have, regardless of the type. Expectations are actions I expect my man to portray. Basically, they represent how I want to be treated by my man. This rule can get a little tricky. Let your expectations be known early in the relationship. Tell him what you like and dislike, so that there is little room for unnecessary drama.

Having expectations for how a man should treat you is a must. Having expectations for the relationship is a recipe for disaster. When you meet a man, you really have no idea what role he is going to play in your life. He may not make it past the first date. So don't expect him to treat you like his woman, if that is not your role in his life. Expectations within the relationship are going to change over time, depending on what the roles are. Take your time, and let the relationship grow, and adjust your expectations for the relationship accordingly.

This is a section in the Rules of Engagement that is going to be based on what actions that YOU like and dislike, not me. I have my own. These are my personal Expectations:

Number One: **I expect my mate or potential mate to tell the truth**. Matter of fact, I expect everyone to tell the truth. Please be honest with me in the beginning about how many women you may or may not be juggling. Let it be my choice to decide if I am going to stay around. I respect honesty and detest habitual liars, so keep it one hundred. Every man has a woman lingering around somewhere in his life; an ex-wife, a baby mama, or a friend with benefits. Telling lies to someone takes away the other person's choices and has the potential for drama, because eventually you will get caught, so you may as well be honest up front.

Number Two: **Please do not come by my house unannounced.** That is just plain rude and disrespectful.

Number Three: **I like to be courted and to go out on dates**. No, you cannot come over to my house and just "chill" and I just met you. I don't know you like that.

Number Four: **If you want to be my man, then you have to step up to the plate**. If I have a need or a problem, and you want the role of my man, then help me come up with a solution. Eldrige Cleaver said it best, *"You are either part of the solution or part of the problem."*

Number Five: **I don't like being ignored and I have stringent phone etiquette**. If I take time to call a man and he does not answer, then I expect a return phone call in a timely fashion. Especially, if the man is trying to get the role of "My Man." He has no idea why I am calling. I could be just calling to hear his voice, or in serious need of help. Please don't blow me off with a text message if it can be avoided.

Number Six: **Please respect my time**. If I have plans to have dinner with a date at 7:00 pm, then that is what time I plan on eating. If by some reason, that time is not going to work, then call and reschedule. Don't make an executive decision as if my opinion does not matter. Also, I do have a life; career, children, family, etc so last minute plans most likely are not going to work. Now that does not mean that I am not flexible. If there is an opportunity to attend a concert or play at the last minute, then of course I can make accommodations.

Number Seven: **Call and check up on me**. Ask me how my day is going. Especially if we have not talked in a while because this lets me know that you are thinking about me and that you care. Let me know that you are still interested in dating me. Keep the lines of communication open.

Number Eight: **I love handy men**. It is so sexy to see a man put on his tool belt or pick his tool box up and go fix something. Now I am not saying that you have to be Bob Villa, but please know how to use tools. It's comforting to know that your man can fix almost anything.

Number Nine: **No nagging**. If I do or say something to you that offends you, or gives you any kind of displeasure, then please talk to me like an adult and tell me what the issue is, so that we can come up with a solution.

No man is going to treat you the way that you want to be treated without some kind of conditioning (training). Now some men may require a lot of training, and some will be minimal. Trust me when I tell you that a man is going to condition us on how he wants to be treated, and we, as women, are typically nurturing creatures, so we will comply to meet his needs to keep him happy. The same theory can be applied in reverse.

A wise man once told me that women should set parameters on how a man should treat her. This has to be a subtle process. This is where the skill of being a Furniture Mover is going to come into play. Three key notes to keep in your mind are: 1) It takes one week to form a habit, 2) three weeks to break one and 3) people notice what is missing when it is gone more than they will notice what was there to begin with.

Think about it. If you convey to a man how important communication is and how promptly that you would like your phone calls returned, and he consistently does not call back in a timely manner, then stop giving him that consideration. The next time that he calls, don't immediately call him back, like you would typically do. Instead of fussing at him about why he takes his time to return your calls, don't return his call at all. Let him call you again. And when he asks you why you didn't call him back so soon, like you always do, politely point out the unwritten Rules of Engagement that he changed with his actions by not respecting your wishes.

Say something like, "What's wrong with that? I had no idea that you wanted your calls returned so promptly. I can only act in the same manner which you present to me. Perhaps we should both make an effort from now on to follow that rule."

If you feel like your "goods" are being taken for granted, then pull back. If the man really cares about you, then he will adapt and change his ways. Men, like women, learn differently. Some men learn by talking, and most learn by showing (actions). Hence the phrase "Actions speak louder than words." There are going to be times when you have to take on the "I can show you better than I can tell you" persona.

Your boundaries and expectations are there for a reason, so use them. The "Boundaries and Expectations" discussion is one that a woman and man should have early on in the infancy stage of the relationship. Unfortunately women are most like going to have to take the lead and initiate and plan the conversation. Please don't hold your breath and wait on a man to approach with this subject, because you will surely pass out. The male mind just does not work like that.

Do not plan to have your "talk" any time during any sports-related event. For example: If your man is on his way out the door to go watch the football game, the last thing that he wants to do is talk to you about anything, let alone his feelings or your feelings. He is way too focused on the game. Or, if he is dealing with anything else emotionally, like the death of a close friend or family member, or problems at his job, all you are going to get is resistance and maybe an argument. Most likely, during this time he is in his "Man Cave" and is not listening to a word that you are saying, so don't waste your breath trying to have a "talk." Instead, pick a time when you and he are both in a relaxed mood and you have his full attention.

The key to boundaries and expectations is knowing who you are on the inside. Once you get to know your inner self, your desires, needs, morals, etc., it will become almost impossible for you to allow someone to come in and hurt you. You will smell b.s. and drama from a mile away and have the wherewithal to flee. The ability to develop and enforce your boundaries takes practice, time, and patience. It is not easy, yet it can be done.

CONSEQUENCES

Consequences

"Consequences give us the pain that motivates us to change." Henry Cloud

Most negative actions should have consequences. When you feel as though a man has displayed some unsportsmanlike conduct by breaking one of the Rules of Engagement, there has got to be a consequence of some sort. Now this can be a doubled edged sword, so watch yourselves ladies, because it can easily come back on you. Negative actions are subjective and depend on your tolerance level. They range anywhere from deal breakers to non-issues.

Consequences can also range from minor to major. Minor: A verbal warning, such as "In the future can you please refrain from coming over to my house and just honking the horn for me to come out? I find that repulsive and totally disrespectful. Now, I don't know what kind of women that you normally date, but I will not put up with that!" Or if the action is severe, try putting the man into what I like to call: T.C.I.

Total
Communication
Isolation

Otherwise known as "the verbal hole." This means no phone calls, text messages, email, Facebook, Twitter, etc. Some men are not worth your time, energy, or words, and it's okay not to share. You see, silence gives a man time to think about the actions that got him put in the hole, and what he should do or not to do in the future in order to stay out of the hole. The same rule can apply in the dating realm.

When you tell a man that you do not want to talk to him, then be firm in your decision, and don't entertain him until you are ready. Like my brother says, "Most men are going to try and get back in your good graces soon. Usually, before you are ready to talk to them, so make them wait until you are ready." A man would rather have you cuss them out than not talk to them at all. In their male minds, they justify it by saying "at least she is talking to me."

Before you put a man in T.C.I. spend some time deciding if what the man did was a deal breaker or a non-issue. Handle the situation like an adult, even if he is not acting like one, and talk to him about why you feel the need to keep your words to yourself. Let him know exactly how displeased you are with his actions, and why you find it necessary to take some time out to spend by yourself. Prepare a speech if you have to. This is the one that I use:

"It pains me to have to go through any length of time and not be able to talk to you; however at this point I am convinced by your actions that it is time for me to do some internal evaluations of myself and this relationship. I will be in my quiet time for an indefinite length of time. Take care and we will talk soon."

The speech is short and to the point. I get my point across in a non-condescending way. I leave the door of communication open. I am letting the man know that I am not happy, making it clear to him that it was his actions, or lack thereof, that gave me the nudge to go into quiet time. The amount of time that a man spends in T.C.I. is up to you.

Some people have a hard time understanding and having empathy for certain situations because they don't understand the dynamics. They lack certain life experience to understand the importance. Often this leads to a feeling of, "It ain't me," or "That's on them." It's unfortunate that the only way to get your point across is to put a person in the same situation. Then all of a sudden the blinders come off, and almost miraculously there is a better understanding of the severity of what is going on. Shame on them! A hard head leads to a soft behind.

DAMAGE CONTROL

Damage Control

"I was deficient in my emotional maturity."
B. Louise Penny

In the dating game there may be times when, as a woman, you are going to find yourself in a negative situation or circumstance that may result in your acting in a negative way. Those negative actions will necessitate your doing some damage control. There is nothing wrong with saying, "I'm Sorry. I was deficient in my emotional maturity." These words are so simple and yet so hard to say. Some men are just going to rub you the wrong way and ignite an unpleasant response. You are going to have to go to that man, apologize, and make amends.

'Fess up and admit when you are wrong, the same way that you boldly go before God and apologize to him, and ask for forgiveness for being disobedient. It is not always the easiest thing to do, especially when you feel as though you have been wronged by him first. Apologizing is a sign of one's emotional maturity and integrity. Be the bigger person and if the person that you are apologizing to does not accept your apology, then that is between that person and God. Apologizing to men is a little tricky. They are not like women, and their minds do not handle emotions very well, so you have to talk in their language. With that being said, here are some basic tips on how to apologize to a man.

Number One: **Don't approach a man when he is distracted or busy.** Trying to talk to him during a sporting event or while he is fixing his car is going to give you both a headache.

81

Number Two: **Plan your approach; set the scene.** Think about what you are going to say beforehand. Write it down and practice if you have to.

Number Three: **Own up to your mistake.** Most, not all men, will respect this type of approach. Men usually prefer to face conflict head-on. However, do not mistake his willingness to resolve an issue quickly with wanting to communicate.

Number Four: **Men like to talk in a direct and plain language so talk straight.** Keep in mind that the male mind only processes one emotion at a time. During an apology is not the time to use excessive words or metaphors. Make sure that your apology is to the point and concise.

Number Five: **Don't point out the man's mistakes or defects during your apology.** Don't try to suggest that he was the one who was actually in the wrong. Most men are naturally ego-driven, and when a man is faced with some kind of conflict, he will retreat once again into his Man Cave until it is safe to come out. Pointing out his shortcomings will not help; it will make him defensive and you will take a chance of resurrecting the argument.

Number Six: **Avoid overreacting**. Make a serious effort not to overreact or make a big deal out of the situation when you approach the man. Overreacting with theatrics will only make him feel uncomfortable and confused. Don't blow the situation out of proportion, because it might cause your gut to feel as if the hurt was deeper than he thought. Most men will usually brush the situation off as a random occurrence, if it is treated as if it weren't that big of a deal to begin with.

Number Seven: **Go public.** If you really messed up then don't be ashamed to apologize in front of other people. This type of public display will stroke any man's ego.

Nobody is perfect and everybody makes mistakes, so don't be afraid to own up to yours when you do. The man that you are dating should understand that you are human and therefore are going to make mistakes. He should accept your apology, and if he doesn't then move on, because it's obvious that he is not your King.

CHAPTER 6

TIPS ON HOW TO MEND A BROKEN HEART

Tips on How to Mend a Broken Heart

"He heals the brokenhearted and binds up their wounds." Psalm 147:3 NIV

Having your heart broken by someone you love can be painful. It is something that most people experience at some point in their lives at least once. There are going to be times when you are going to get your heart broken and there are going to be times when you are going to be the heart breaker. Both situations can be emotionally draining.

There is no medication that a doctor can subscribe to mend a broken heart. Once you give someone access to your heart, they have an open pass to everything you are. Your mind, body and emotions start with your heart. It is the core of who you are as a person. That's why it is so important to safeguard your heart and enter a relationship slowly with your eyes wide open.

Don't let a past relationship that ended in heartache for you discourage you from allowing yourself to love again. The following are universal tips that I have learned over the years.

Number One: **Pray about it and give the situation to God**. In essence, let go and let God take over. Don't worry about it anymore and get your peace back.

Number Two: **Love from a distance**. My Aunt Janie, may she rest in peace, used to tell me that all the time. It's okay to love people, even the ones who hurt you. Some people you just have to love from a distance. Emotionally, "check out" of the relationship. Loving someone who hurt you emotionally does not make you weak, it makes you human.

Number Three: **Get out the house.** Don't stay at home crying and waiting for the phone to ring. Get out the house and enjoy yourself. Call your girlfriends, or spend more time with your family. Start a hobby or join a book club. Keep yourself busy.

Number Four: **Keep your appearance up**. Make sure to eat and stay well groomed. The best "revenge" is looking good and being happy. Do something extra nice for yourself. Manicures, pedicures, massages, or a make-over, and if you happen to run into Mr. Man out in public, then kill him with kindness.

Number Five: **It is what it is**. Examine the relationship for what it really was. Ask yourself some tough questions. What was your part in the situation? What did you learn? What are you going to do differently in the future? It's not right, but it is okay, or rather, it's going to be okay. Don't think of the past relationship as something that is ending. Think of it as a beginning of a whole new wiser you.

Number Six: **Respect his wishes**. If an ex-lover tells you not to call him anymore, then do just that. Don't call him, plain and simple. Instead, take care of you and what you have to do. Even if you left some personal belongings at his house, still don't call him. One of two things will happen: He will make arrangements with you to give you back your items, or you won't get them back. Just chalk him and your items up as a loss, because God will bless you with someone new.

Number Seven: **Take your own advice**. Give yourself a pep talk with the same advice that you would give a close friend. Recognize your strengths, and tell yourself that "it's his loss," and move on.

If he broke your heart, he doesn't deserve it. Focus on doing your own thing and enjoy the pleasant surprise or happy accident of falling in love. Respect the serendipity of the love process, and allow yourself to heal before jumping right into a serious relationship with someone else too soon. Sometimes you reach a point in a relationship when you have to let go in order to hold on to your sanity. It's okay to walk away, and it does not mean you don't love that person anymore. It means that you love yourself enough to walk away. Learn from your experience, and don't make the same mistakes in your next relationship.

SECTION SEVEN

YOUR NEXT MOVE

Your Next Move

*"Just because I like it, don't mean that I need it.
Live life fabulous and free."* Vivian Green

God did not create you to be treated like a doormat, or to be stepped and walked all over. Focus on your relationship with God and take care of you. Eventually your King will appear. A wise woman used to tell me all the time that the essence of who we are is in our thought life. If you think that all the men are dogs, then those are the type of men that you are going to keep attracting. Remember to use the tips and mental tools that I shared with you in this playbook to minimize your heartache. My goal in writing the playbook is to inform women on what to do and what not to do in the dating arena.

Let's review the topics discussed in this playbook:

o Take some time and get to know yourself.

o Form your boundaries and expectations and let them be known early in the relationship.

o No boyfriend privileges without boyfriend responsibilities.

o Let the man know in a nonchalant way that he has competition.

o Try to keep your baggage down to a minimum. Forgive and move on.

o Ask those important questions early on in the

relationship.

o   Stay away from emotionally needy men.

o   Do your background check.

o   Don't focus on getting revenge on a man that hurt you. Let Karma come and claim her prize.

o   Men will tell you what they think your worth is by their actions towards you.

o   Be watchful for Red Flags.

o   Stay away from Bottom Feeders.

o   Some people are not worth your time, energy, or words.

o   Never make a man a priority when he only makes you an option. Recognize by his actions when he tries to put you on the back burner. If a man is truly in love with you, then he will make it a point to keep you happy all the time, not just when it's convenient for him.

Take your relationships with men one day at a time. If or when God decides to touch that mans' heart and whisper in his ear that you are the woman for him, then he will make the provisions to ensure that you won't go anywhere. The core of any romantic relationship should be their friendship, and the best relationships are built on a friendship that develops into love over time. Don't get so wrapped up in hoping that the relationship is going to work out. Keep your guard up and don't kiss too many frogs in the process of looking for a mate.

KayCee Sherrelle currently resides in Kansas City, Missouri with her three children. *She's Got Game, The Playbook* is her first published book and she is presently writing her second book. For ordering information please visit www.amazon.com.